Learn by Handwriting

Practice Workbook

Print 2

United States of America
States and Capitals

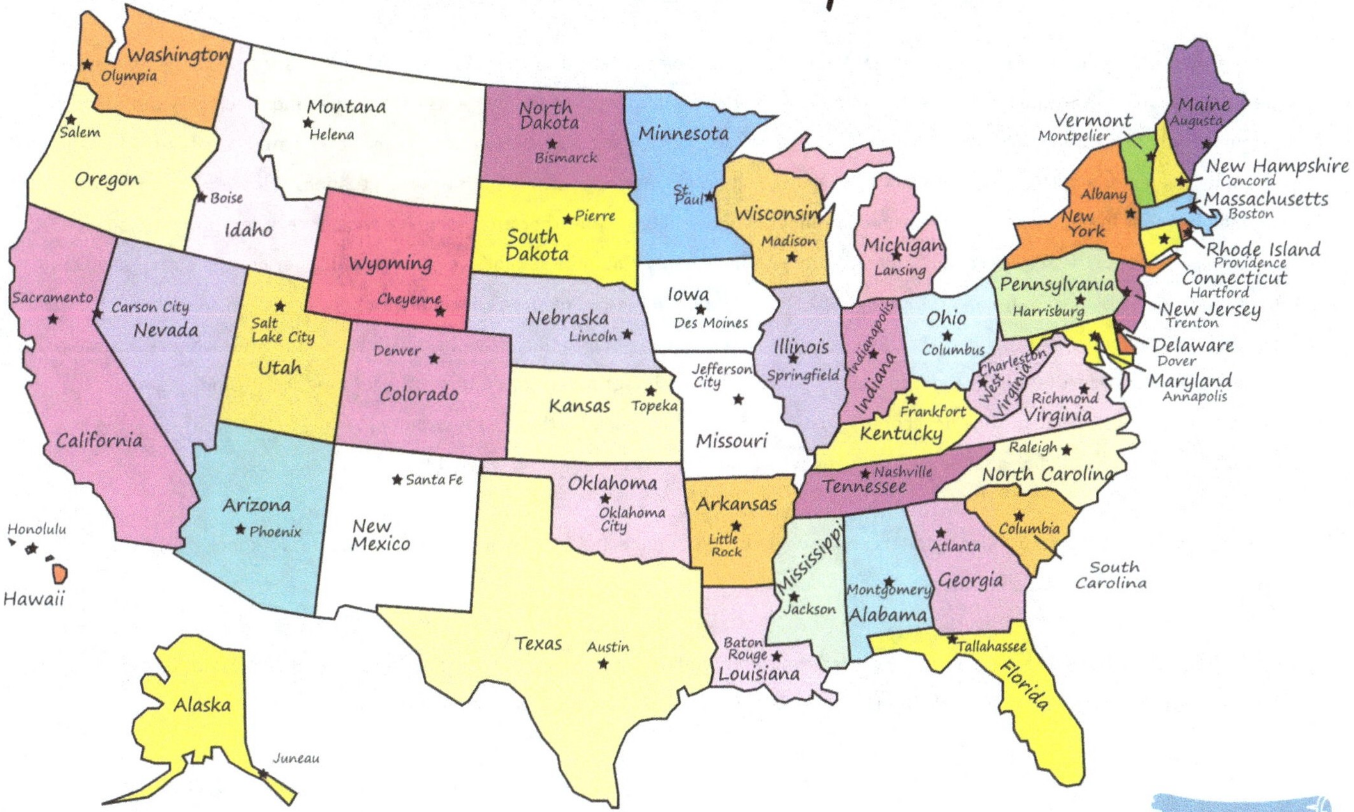

TABLE OF CONTENTS

Dearest Persevering Writer,

One of my proudest achievements at the age of 8 was learning to read and write in cursive. Learning cursive whisked me away on adventures as I read my grandparents' beautiful handwritten travel postcards. Even today, I cherish my grandmother's handwritten recipe card as well as her personalized book inscriptions that I have the chance to re-read as I pass those books along to my children.

Many of us can remember the time before handwriting was eclipsed by digital communication. Consider the present reality, all the text messages and emails we read but barely remember and rarely keep as a treasured memory. While there are innumerable benefits to computer use and digital communication, handwriting remains a powerful, valuable skill.

Memorescribe Learn by Handwriting workbooks began as a passion project. When working to help my child develop handwriting skills, I discovered an opportunity to use handwriting practice time to learn and reinforce important educational information. Memorescribe workbooks offer you the opportunity to practice and develop your personal, unique handwriting style while taking advantage of the time to learn something new or reinforce information you learned in the past.

Wherever you are on your journey, no matter your age or handwriting ability, my hope is that Memorescribe's Learn by Handwriting workbooks will send you off on your own learning adventures, travelling as far as your handwriting will take you.

Jessica

Welcome to Memorescribe

Memorescribe Learn by Handwriting workbooks create a fun and meaningful opportunity to commit educational information to memory while you practice your handwriting because we believe handwriting is an invaluable skill. **Learn as you write with Memorescribe!**

IMPORTANCE OF HANDWRITING

1. Writing by hand is a **foundational educational skill** connected to academic progress and success.

2. Writing by hand **activates** different parts of **the brain** and can **boost** your **brain function**.

3. Writing by hand helps to **develop** the **small movements** and **coordination skills** needed **for success in everyday life**.

4. Handwriting notes helps to **organize thoughts** and **process information** more **deeply** which can lead to **better learning**, understanding, **retaining**, and recalling **information**.

5. A unique form of personal expression, handwriting can **display individual personality**, creative tendencies, and artistic craftsmanship as well as **verify identity**.

6. Writing by hand can help to **process emotions**, **set goals**, soothe and calm while encouraging **personal reflection** on experiences and circumstances.

7. Handwritten notes and documents convey a **memorable**, meaningful, **personal touch** and **demonstrate care** and thoughtfulness towards the recipient.

8. Preserving methods and styles of handwriting allows people groups and cultures the opportunity to **maintain heritage** and **safeguard history**.

Print and Cursive Handwriting

Print Handwriting, also known as Manuscript, is patterned after the style of letters commonly used in printed materials such as books, newspapers, or magazines. Each letter is written independently and is not connected to any other letter. To create print style handwriting, the writer lifts the pen or pencil from the paper after forming each letter. Print handwriting is simple and can often be easier to read than cursive style writing.

Cursive Handwriting is also known as Script, longhand, or joined-up writing. The scripted style of writing is created using connected, flowing letters which allows for faster, more elegant writing than print. Writers of cursive use single strokes to create letters without lifting the pen or pencil from the paper and connect the letters within the same word. Cursive handwriting is more intricate than print and can add a touch of sophistication whenever used.

With **Memorescribe,** *you can choose your handwriting style and text size.* For handwriting style, choose between print and cursive. For handwriting text size, choose from level 1, level 2, or level 3 in your selected style.

Workbooks are available in the following style and size options:

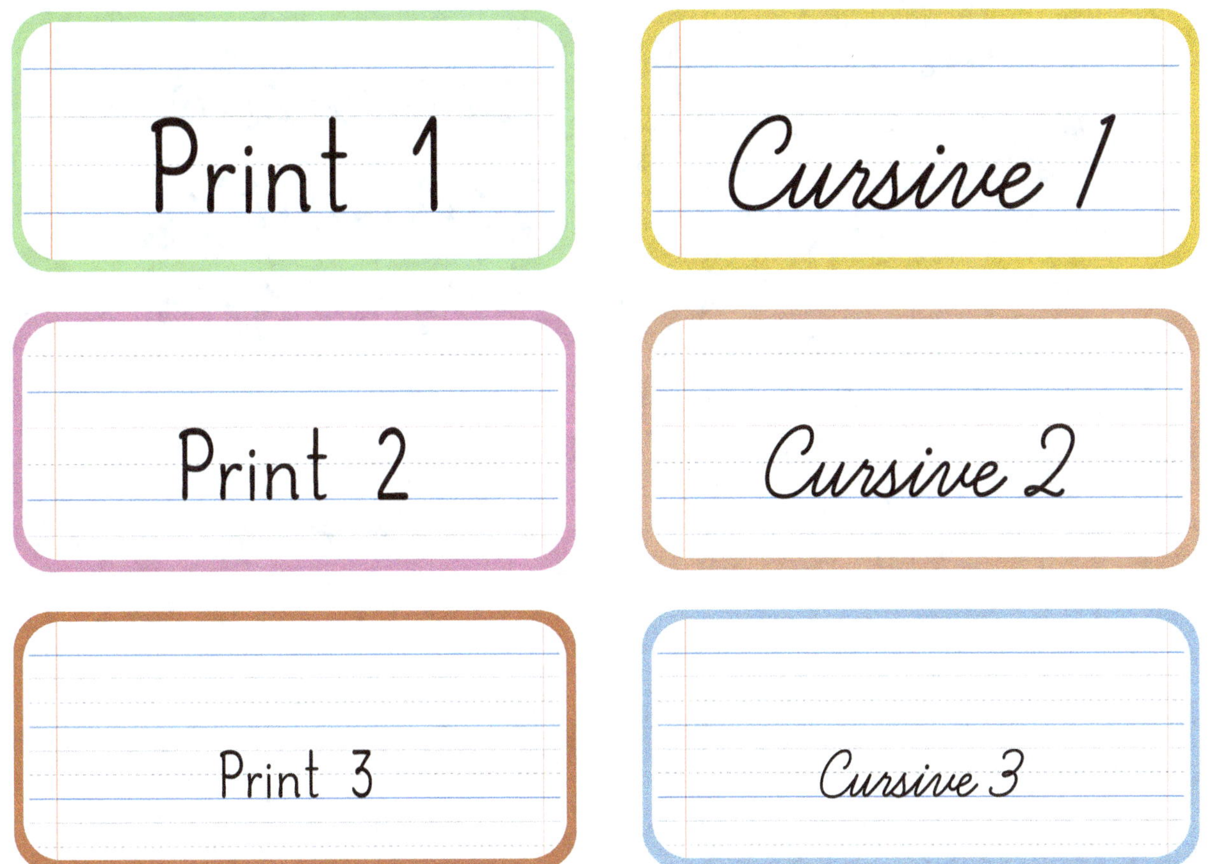

Books available in English, Spanish, and other languages.

Recommendations for Comfortable Handwriting

Pencil Grip Tip:

Pinch the pencil between your thumb and first finger. Rest the pinched fingers with pencil on the middle finger. Curl the last two fingers into the palm of your hand for support as you rest your hand on the writing surface.

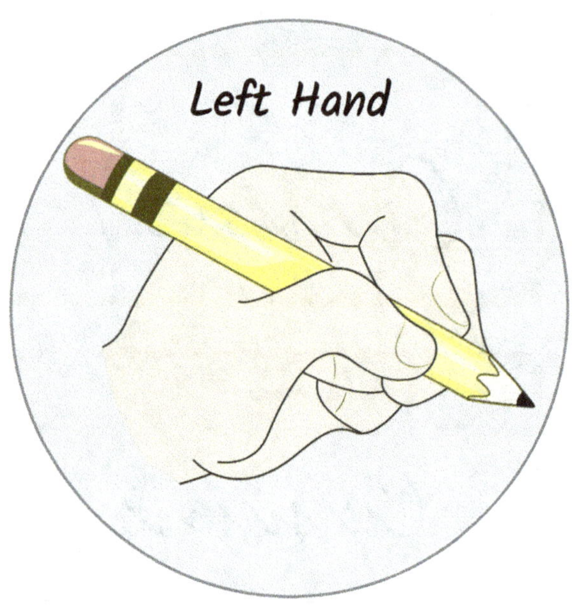

Supportive Handwriting Pencil Grip

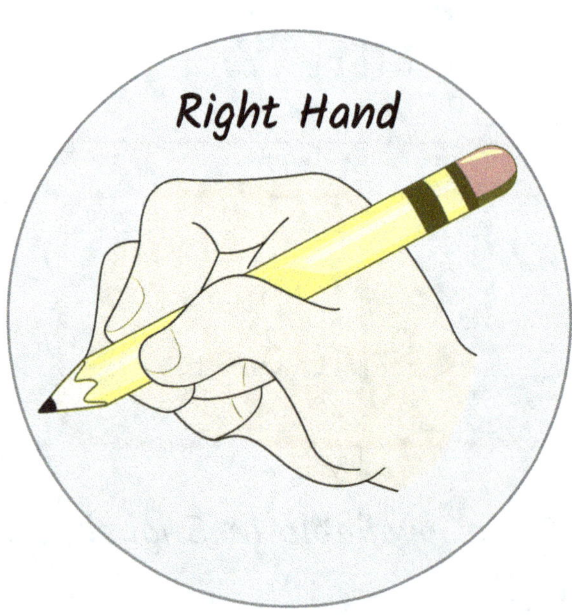

PRACTICE MAKES THE MASTER

Part 1

STATE	POSTAL ABBREVIATION	CAPITAL	FLAG
Alabama	AL	Montgomery	
Alaska	AK	Juneau	
Arizona	AZ	Phoenix	
Arkansas	AR	Little Rock	
California	CA	Sacramento	
Colorado	CO	Denver	
Connecticut	CT	Hartford	
Delaware	DE	Dover	
Florida	FL	Tallahassee	
Georgia	GA	Atlanta	

Alabama, Montgomery, AL

Alabama became the 22nd state on December 14, 1819.

Alabama, Montgomery, AL

Alaska, Juneau, AK

Alaska became the 49th state on January 3, 1959.

Alaska, Juneau, AK

United States of America – States and Capitals

memorescribe.com

Arizona, Phoenix, AZ

Arizona became the 48th state on February 14, 1912.

Arizona, Phoenix, AZ

Arkansas, Little Rock, AR

 Arkansas became the 25th state on June 15, 1836.

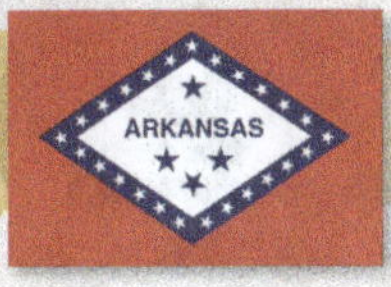

State: **Arkansas,** Capital: **Little Rock,** State Abbreviation: **AR**

Arkansas, Little Rock, AR

In 1962, Sam Walton opened his first Wal-Mart store in Rogers, **Arkansas**, called Wal-Mart Discount City.

California, Sacramento, CA

California became the 31st state on September 9, 1850.

California, Sacramento, CA

United States of America – States and Capitals

memorescribe.com

Colorado, Denver, CO

   Colorado became the 38th state on August 1, 1876.

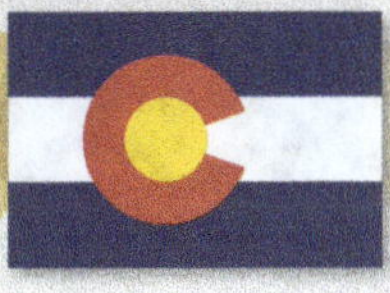

Colorado, Denver, CO

1

2

3

4

5

6

7

8

9

10

11

12

13

Connecticut, Hartford, CT

1

2

3

4

5

6

7

8

9

10

11

12

13

 Connecticut became the 5th state on January 9, 1788.

State: **Connecticut,** Capital: **Hartford,** State Abbreviation: **CT**

Connecticut, Hartford, CT

The Wadsworth Atheneum in Hartford, **Connecticut**, which opened in 1844, is the oldest U.S. public art museum.

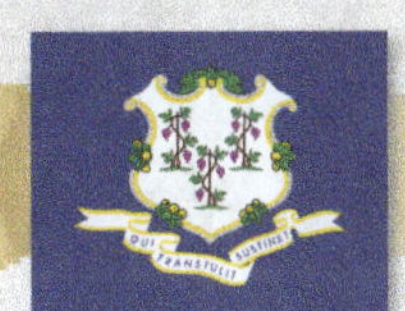

Delaware, Dover, DE

Delaware became the 1st state on December 7, 1787.

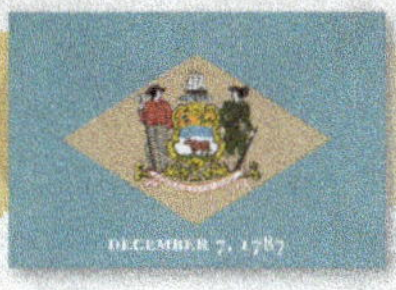

State: **Delaware,** Capital: **Dover,** State Abbreviation: **DE**

Delaware, Dover, DE

Delaware was the first state to ratify the federal Constitution on December 7, 1787.

Florida, Tallahassee, FL

Florida became the 27th state on March 3, 1845.

Florida, Tallahassee, FL

Georgia, Atlanta, GA

Georgia became the 4th state on January 2, 1788.

Georgia, Atlanta, GA

Directions:

Search to find the list of words hidden inside the puzzle. Words can go in any direction and share letters.

```
C X F D A R D H W B A D F S
A O H L H Q E A Y L Z R L A
Y F L K A U J V A A O O O S
A A Z O A D A S N D V F R N
D O V E R I K O D E O T I A
X Z N S G A Z T X L D R D K
J U M R Q I D I F A N A A R
J G O N R V E O P W R H D A
W E X A Q A V F F A J X U R
G A T L A N T A O R X P P C
X Q M T U C I T C E N N O C
E E S S A H A L L A T J C X
X Q L I T T L E R O C K Y S
O T N E M A R C A S Q J U U
```

COLORADO FLORIDA ALASKA DOVER

ARIZONA ATLANTA DELAWARE HARTFORD

JUNEAU LITTLE ROCK SACRAMENTO ARKANSAS

DENVER TALLAHASSEE CONNECTICUT GEORGIA

Part 2

STATE	POSTAL ABBREVIATION	CAPITAL	FLAG
Hawaii	HI	Honolulu	
Idaho	ID	Boise	
Illinois	IL	Springfield	
Indiana	IN	Indianapolis	
Iowa	IA	Des Moines	
Kansas	KS	Topeka	
Kentucky	KY	Frankfort	
Louisiana	LA	Baton Rouge	
Maine	ME	Augusta	
Maryland	MD	Annapolis	

Hawaii, Honolulu, HI

Hawaii became the 50th state on August 21, 1959.

Hawaii, Honolulu, HI

1

2

3

4

5

6

7

8

9

10

11

12

13

Idaho, Boise, ID

Idaho became the 43rd state on July 3, 1890.

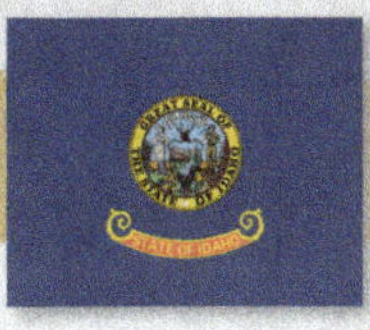

State: **Idaho**, Capital: **Boise**, State Abbreviation: **ID**

Idaho, Boise, ID

Hells Canyon, the deepest gorge in North America, forms part of the **Idaho**-Oregon state boundary.

Illinois, Springfield, IL

 Illinois became the 21st state on December 3, 1818.

Illinois, Springfield, IL

The Sears Tower in Chicago, **Illinois**, was the world's tallest building from 1974 until 1996.

Indiana, Indianapolis, IN

Indiana became the 19th state on December 11, 1816.

Indiana, Indianapolis, IN

Iowa, Des Moines, IA

   Iowa became the 29th state on December 28, 1846.

Iowa, Des Moines, IA

Kansas, Topeka, KS

1

2

3

4

5

6

7

8

9

10

11

12

13

   Kansas became the 34th state on January 29, 1861.

Kansas, Topeka, KS

Kentucky, Frankfort, KY

Kentucky became the 15th state on June 1, 1792.

Kentucky, Frankfort, KY

Louisiana, Baton Rouge, LA

Louisiana became the 18th state on April 30, 1812.

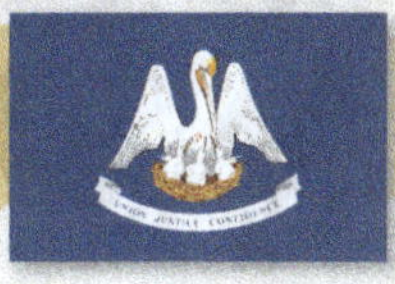

State: **Louisiana**, Capital: **Baton Rouge**, State Abbreviation: **LA**

Louisiana, Baton Rouge, LA

The main celebration for the world-famous "Mardi Gras" takes place in New Orleans, **Louisiana**.

Maine, Augusta, ME

 Maine became the 23rd state on March 15, 1820.

Maine, Augusta, ME

Maryland, Annapolis, MD

memorescribe.com

United States of America - States and Capitals

© Globaloft, LLC

Maryland became the 7th state on April 28, 1788.

Maryland, Annapolis, MD

1

2

3

4

5

6

7

8

9

10

11

12

13

Directions: Use the clues below to discover the missing words. Words share letters where they cross in the puzzle.

ACROSS

2. The capital city of The Aloha State, Hawaii...

7. Home to Indianapolis and the world's largest children's museum...

8. State whose capital Annapolis is home to the U.S. Naval Academy...

9. The Sunflower State, capital Topeka...

10. State sharing a border with Canada to the North, capital Boise...

DOWN

1. Frankfort is the capital of The Bluegrass State...

3. State whose capital is Baton Rouge, meaning "red stick"...

4. The capital of Maine, a state famous for its lobster...

5. This state's capital is Des Moines...

6. This state is surrounded by water on all sides...

Part 3

STATE	POSTAL ABBREVIATION	CAPITAL	FLAG
Massachusetts	MA	Boston	
Michigan	MI	Lansing	
Minnesota	MN	Saint Paul	
Mississippi	MS	Jackson	
Missouri	MO	Jefferson City	
Montana	MT	Helena	
Nebraska	NE	Lincoln	
Nevada	NV	Carson City	
New Hampshire	NH	Concord	
New Jersey	NJ	Trenton	

Massachusetts, Boston, MA

Massachusetts became the 6th state on February 6, 1788.

Massachusetts, Boston, MA

Michigan, Lansing, MI

Michigan became the 26th state on January 26, 1837.

Michigan, Lansing, MI

Minnesota, Saint Paul, MN

Minnesota became the 32nd state on May 11, 1858.

Minnesota, Saint Paul, MN

Mississippi, Jackson, MS

    Mississippi became the 20th state on December 10, 1817.

Mississippi, Jackson, MS

Missouri, Jefferson City, MO

Missouri became the 24th state on August 10, 1812.

Missouri, Jefferson City, MO

Montana, Helena, MT

     Montana became the 41st state on November 8, 1889.

Montana, Helena, MT

Nebraska, Lincoln, NE

Nebraska became the 37th state on March 1, 1867.

Nebraska, Lincoln, NE

Nevada, Carson City, NV

Nevada became the 36th state on October 31, 1864.

Nevada, Carson City, NV

New Hampshire, Concord, NH

New Hampshire became the 9th state on June 21, 1788.

New Hampshire, Concord, NH

New Hampshire is the birthplace of Alan B. Shepard, Jr., the first U.S. astronaut to travel to space.

New Jersey, Trenton, NJ

New Jersey became the 3rd state on December 18, 1787.

New Jersey, Trenton, NJ

Directions: Use the clues to decode each word in the puzzle. Then use the numbered letters in the decoded words to discover the hidden puzzle at the bottom.

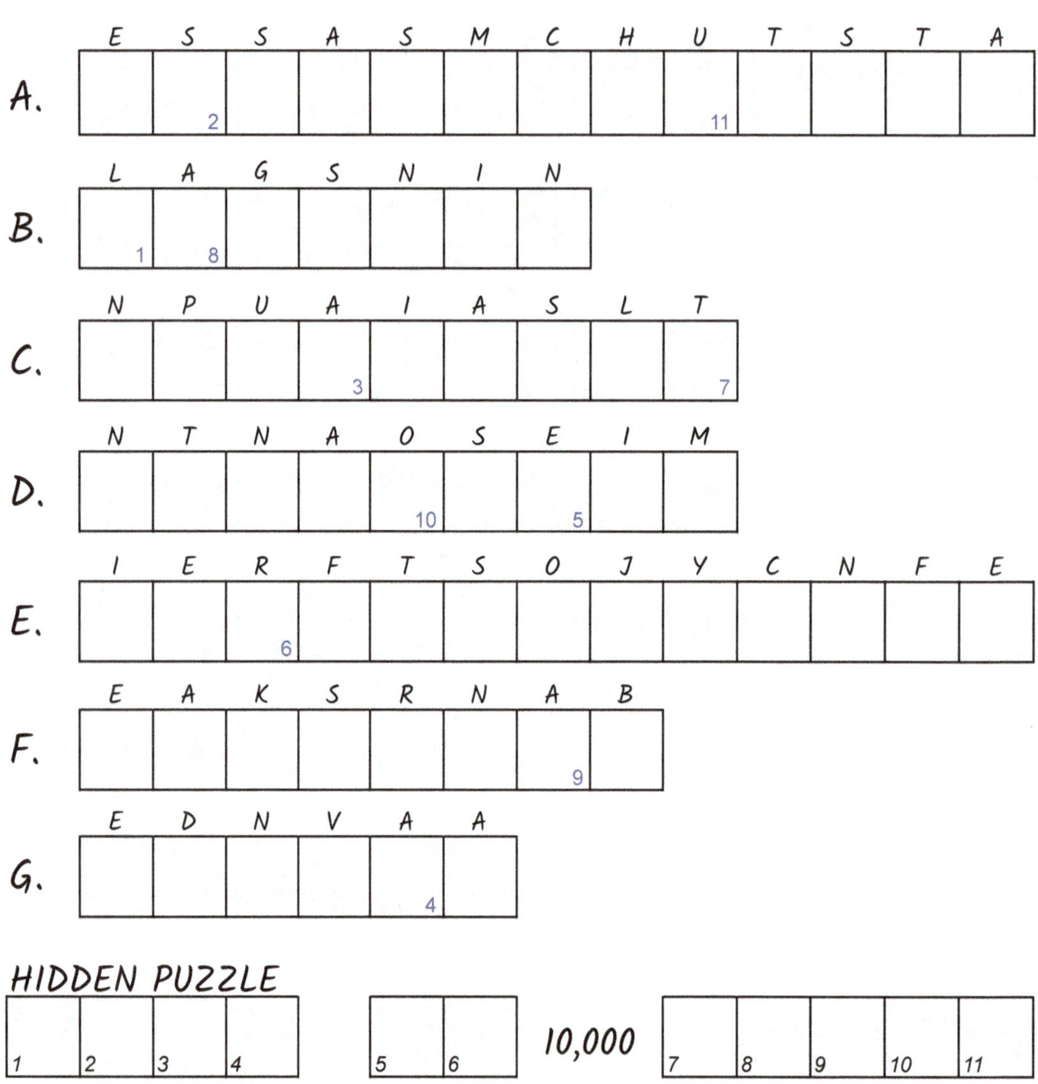

CLUES

A. Home of the first Thanksgiving, capital Boston...

B. Capital of Michigan, state touching 4 Great Lakes...

C. Capital of Minnesota, start of the Mississippi River...

D. State with Twin Cities Minneapolis and Saint Paul...

E. Capital of Missouri, home to the Gateway Arch...

F. State capital Lincoln, named after Abraham Lincoln...

G. State producing the most gold, capital Carson City...

HIDDEN PUZZLE CLUE: Nickname for Minnesota...

Part 4

STATE	POSTAL ABBREVIATION	CAPITAL	FLAG
New Mexico	NM	Santa Fe	
New York	NY	Albany	
North Carolina	NC	Raleigh	
North Dakota	ND	Bismarck	
Ohio	OH	Columbus	
Oklahoma	OK	Oklahoma City	
Oregon	OR	Salem	
Pennsylvania	PA	Harrisburg	
Rhode Island	RI	Providence	
South Carolina	SC	Columbia	

New Mexico, Santa Fe, NM

New Mexico became the 47th state on January 6, 1912.

State: **New Mexico,** Capital: **Santa Fe,** State Abbreviation: **NM**

New Mexico, Santa Fe, NM

New York, Albany, NY

New York became the 11th state on July 26, 1788.

New York, Albany, NY

North Carolina, Raleigh, NC

North Carolina became the 12th state on November 21, 1789.

North Carolina, Raleigh, NC

North Dakota, Bismarck, ND

North Dakota became the 39th state on November 2, 1889.

North Dakota, Bismarck, ND

Ohio, Columbus, OH

Ohio became the 17th state on March 1, 1803.

Ohio, Columbus, OH

1

2

3

4

5

6

7

8

9

10

11

12

13

Oklahoma, Oklahoma City, OK

Oklahoma became the 46th state on November 16, 1907.

State: **Oklahoma**, Capital: **Oklahoma City**, State Abbreviation: **OK**

Oklahoma, Oklahoma City, OK

The **Oklahoma** State Capitol is located on top of a working oil field, surrounded by active oil rigs.

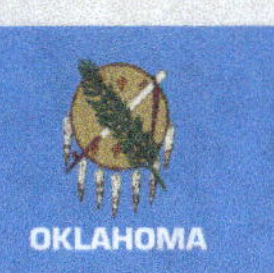

Oregon, Salem, OR

Oregon became the 33rd state on February 14, 1859.

Oregon, Salem, OR

Crater Lake in **Oregon**, measuring 1,943 feet deep, is the deepest lake in the United States.

Pennsylvania, Harrisburg, PA

Pennsylvania became the 2nd state on December 12, 1787.

Pennsylvania, Harrisburg, PA

Rhode Island, Providence, RI

Rhode Island, Providence, RI

South Carolina, Columbia, SC

South Carolina became the 8th state on May 23, 1788.

South Carolina, Columbia, SC

Break Activity 4
Word Search

Directions:

Search to find the list of words hidden inside the puzzle.
Words can go in any direction and share letters.

```
J  R  N  D  O  N  W  M  D  K  E  B  G  C
K  A  L  L  Z  Z  E  D  E  U  D  R  R  O
A  L  B  A  N  Y  K  W  O  L  U  O  C  L
C  E  X  E  E  T  K  H  Y  B  A  I  N  U
O  I  F  H  F  F  I  C  S  O  X  S  O  M
L  G  A  X  A  O  U  I  R  E  R  Q  G  B
U  H  T  L  T  U  R  B  M  A  K  K  E  U
M  C  X  B  N  R  J  W  G  Y  M  O  R  S
B  P  S  Y  A  P  E  Q  Y  L  Q  S  O  Q
I  N  V  H  S  N  T  K  E  E  Y  G  I  Z
A  N  I  L  O  R  A  C  H  T  R  O  N  B
A  Z  N  O  R  T  H  D  A  K  O  T  A  N
A  M  O  H  A  L  K  O  E  P  J  H  I  Z
P  E  N  N  S  Y  L  V  A  N  I  A  I  S
```

ALBANY	COLUMBUS	NEW YORK	OHIO
SANTA FE	OREGON	BISMARCK	HARRISBURG
OKLAHOMA	RALEIGH	COLUMBIA	SALEM
NEW MEXICO	NORTH DAKOTA	PENNSYLVANIA	NORTH CAROLINA

Part 5

STATE	POSTAL ABBREVIATION	CAPITAL	FLAG
South Dakota	SD	Pierre	
Tennessee	TN	Nashville	
Texas	TX	Austin	
Utah	UT	Salt Lake City	
Vermont	VT	Montpelier	
Virginia	VA	Richmond	
Washington	WA	Olympia	
West Virginia	WV	Charleston	
Wisconsin	WI	Madison	
Wyoming	WY	Cheyenne	

South Dakota, Pierre, SD

South Dakota became the 40th state on November 2, 1889.

South Dakota, Pierre, SD

Tennessee, Nashville, TN

Tennessee became the 16th state on June 1, 1796.

Tennessee, Nashville, TN

Texas, Austin, TX

Texas became the 28th state on December 29, 1845.

Texas, Austin, TX

Utah, Salt Lake City, UT

Utah became the 45th state on January 4, 1896.

Utah, Salt Lake City, UT

Vermont, Montpelier, VT

Vermont became the 14th state on March 4, 1791.

Vermont, Montpelier, VT

Vermont is the largest producer of maple syrup in the United States.

Virginia, Richmond, VA

Virginia became the 10th state on June 25, 1788.

Virginia, Richmond, VA

Washington, Olympia, WA

Washington became the 42nd state on November 11, 1889.

Washington, Olympia, WA

West Virginia, Charleston, WV

West Virginia, Charleston, WV

1

2

3

4

5

6

7

8

9

10

11

12

13

Wisconsin, Madison, WI

Wisconsin became the 30th state on May 29, 1848.

Wisconsin, Madison, WI

Wyoming, Cheyenne, WY

Wyoming became the 44th state on July 10, 1890.

Wyoming, Cheyenne, WY

Break Activities Solutions

PAGE 30

PAGE 74

PAGE 52

PAGE 96

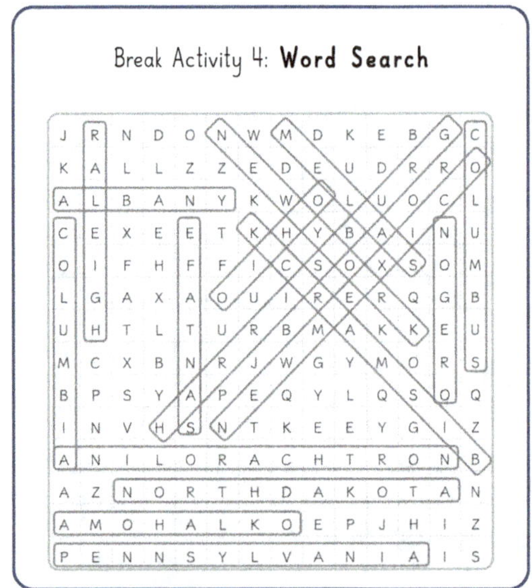

The Memorescribe Advantage

Memorescribe Workbook Themes

Family

Nature

Math

Manners

Faith

Science

World

Sports

General Knowledge

and more to come!

Contact us for customized content for your organization or project.